Renee

I,  is

book beneficial and
Sanctifying.

THE
AMERICAN
MASQUERADE

THE AMERICAN MASQUERADE

AN HONEST CONVERSATION ON AMERICAN CHRISTIANITY

CLAY BRIDGES
PRESS

JOSEPH VINCENT

TABLE OF CONTENTS

INTRODUCTION

A Tribute

I WOULD LIKE TO begin this book with a brief tribute to the conservative denominations and churches of the United States. There are thousands of churches headed by faithful pastors and full of devoted believers all across the nation that love Jesus and stand for His truth. These conservative believers hold to orthodox doctrine and believe in hard work and traditional values. They also love this nation and want to see it prosper and thrive.

I personally come from a long line of these hard-working, bible believing, and traditional Americans. I greatly appreciate my upbringing and the influence my parents, grandparents, and community members have had in my life. I have immense respect for conservative Christians that love their God and their country. This book is written out of love and concern for these people which I owe so much.

I hope, through this book, we can begin an honest conversation about our strengths and our weaknesses. I hope we can set our pride aside. I hope we can be honest about our failures while holding on to the things we've done well. I hope we can open up a dialogue that will lead to a stronger, more loving, and more purposeful church. That is the intention of this book

Where It All Started

On June 26, 2015, a Supreme Court ruling granted recognition to same-sex marriage across the entire nation. Two months later, at 26 years old, I would become the pastor of a small SBC church about an hour North of Dallas. As I'm sure everyone remembers, the following year saw a chaotic presidential campaign that ended with Donald Trump in the White House.

This was obviously a turbulent time to be a new pastor. The liberal movement within the American church was touting the Supreme Court ruling as a victory for love. This same group of people had a disdain for their new president that is too intense to fully describe. However, the professing Christians that were staunch conservatives felt like that fateful day in June marked the end of our freedom as Christians. Many of them also viewed the controversial new Commander in Chief as the savior of western civilization.

There has been a great deal of literature published on the liberal movement within Christianity. It is a real problem and the church should be urged to cling to historical and orthodox doctrine. However, this group is not the target of this book. Being a vocational minister in a conservative denomination, my experience has been with the conservatives, and this is the group this book is meant for. This group of conservative, patriotic, Republican churchgoers that cling to their Christian values shook with fear and burned with anger during this time period. After talking to some of my church members a few months after the court ruling, one might have thought that the Babylonians had just broken down the front gate and were beginning to raid the nation.

Then came Donald Trump. Despite not being known as a religious man, and actually being considered a moral degenerate by many, the conservative religious folks shouted with sheer joy at his presidency. They really felt like this would be the man that would restore order, tear down the altars to Baal, and drag our culture and government back from the darkness.

I pastored that church in North Texas for two years. During those two years, I transformed a great deal. My theology, ecclesiology, eschatology, and other ologies all changed. I guess you could say I am a part of the Young, Restless, and Reformed crowd, but while there will be some evidence of my Reformed theology, this book is not about Reformed theology and is applicable to everyone professing Christ as their Savior, not just Reformed thinkers.

Another thing that changed during this time was my view of the religious conservative right. Watching the aftermath of the Supreme Court decision and observing Bible Belt conservatives during the 2016 presidential campaign at the small local church level brought a lot of things to light that I had not noticed before. The primary revelation was, what I call, the American Masquerade. The American Masquerade summarized is this, in the United States there is a large social and political movement of conservative-minded people, particularly in the South and rural areas, that is masquerading as the church but has no real grasp of the gospel of Jesus Christ or what Christianity actually is.

This is the reason for this book. This book is intended to reveal the masquerade that is the American religious conservative movement. Christianity has been transformed into nothing more than a political and social movement. The church is dedicated to forcing Christian values on its neighbors but teaches nothing of the true gospel, and the government is called upon to preserve the culture because the church cannot stand discomfort or hardship.

If the church is going to be effective, we must recognize where we went wrong, and have the humility to accept correction. We have to remember the Rock we are founded on, Jesus. Jesus is not about making the people around you to look and act like you so that you are comfortable. Jesus is not about you getting and keeping what is "rightfully yours." Jesus is about changing sinner's hearts, rescuing them from their sinfulness, and doing it all for the glory of the trinitarian God of the universe. That is the message of this book so please, read this with a heart wanting to know Jesus, and wanting to serve Him obediently.

I am approaching this issue, not as an academic on the coast looking down his nose at the peasants in the flyover states, but as an associate pastor in an SBC church in a small town in the panhandle of Texas. I have spent my entire life attending or serving in small rural churches in the Bible Belt. My primary goal is for Jesus to be exalted and the church to find its true purpose. I love the people of rural America and I do feel like there is a richness in our culture that we need to hold on to. We work hard, we take care of our neighbors, and respect our elders. But we can't make our traditions and our culture more important than the gospel. We can't turn the church into just a political interest group. We need to return to the true gospel and the true mission of sharing His message and advancing His kingdom, His way.

THE MASK OF MORALITY

THE IDEA OF this book was sparked by a sermon I preached about a year ago. It was entitled, you guessed it, the American Masquerade. The text was Luke 7:36-50.[1] In this passage, Jesus is dining at the home of a Pharisee, and a woman known to be a sinner came into the home and began to wash Jesus' feet. Simon, the Pharisee, scoffed at Jesus allowing this because the woman was a sinner and Jesus was supposed to be a great pious teacher. The story ends with Jesus telling the woman, "Your faith has saved you; go in peace."

Another text that was very influential in this idea, but was not used in the sermon, is Luke 18: 9-14. This is the parable of the tax collector and the Pharisee going to the temple. The Pharisee seemed to pray to God, but in reality, simply sang his own praises to himself. The tax collector was so broken over his sin he could not even

---

[1] ESV 2016

look up. Jesus tells us he was the one made righteous by this visit to the temple.

The Pharisees

Before we get into the exegesis of these texts, it is important to clear up our understanding of a common character the two passages share, the Pharisees. We were all raised to hate these holier than thou religious tyrants. They always heckled Jesus and ultimately murdered him. By the time we were in second or third grade, we had a healthy disgust for the whole lot. What we might not know is we could have more in common with them than we think.

According to Vine's Dictionary, the Pharisees were successors of the Hasidaeans. The Hasidaeans or, pious ones, were a group of religious zealots that were dedicated to God's law. The group was formed in the post-exile era of Israel to combat the increasing threat of Greek culture. Some Jews embraced Hellenization and thought orthodox Judaism to be too narrow. The Hasidaeans however, were committed to separating themselves from anything that was not strictly Jewish. They loved their nation, their ancient teachings, and their culture.

Over the years though, as the Hasidaeans phased out and the Pharisees took their place, they seem to have lost their way. The law, the culture, and the nation became an idol. Vine puts it this way, "In their zeal for the Law they almost deified it and their attitude became merely external, formal, mechanical. They laid stress, not upon the righteousness of action, but upon its formal correctness. Consequently, their opposition to Christ was inevitable; His manner of life and teaching was essentially a condemnation of theirs; hence His denunciation of them."[2] The Pharisees treasured the law of God. While it is a good and right thing to be dedicated to the commands of Scripture, the Pharisees worshiped the Old Testament law to the point that they missed the primary purpose of it.

In the book of Romans, Paul, a former Pharisee, gives a great deal of insight into the function of the law. One of those functions was to make sinful creatures aware of their sinfulness. "I would not have known sin. For I would not have known what it is to covet if the law had not said, 'You shall not covet.'" (Romans 7:7b). The

---

[2] W.E. Vine. Vine's Expository Dictionary of Biblical Words. Nashville, TN. Thomas Nelson Publishers. 1985 (pg. 470

law makes people aware of their natural inclination to disobey and rebel against a holy God that created them.

While the law makes sin known to man, it does not have the ability to rescue man from sin. Paul makes this clear in Romans 3:20, "For by works of the law no human being will be justified in his sight since through the law comes knowledge of sin." The law was designed to first make sin known, then to point the sinner toward salvation. "But now the righteousness of God has been manifested apart from the law, although the Law and the Prophets bear witness to it—the righteousness of God through faith in Jesus Christ for all who believe." (Romans 3:21-22a) The Pharisees made the mistake of viewing the law as a tool of justification. They viewed piety and formal conformity to the law as the means of justification and good standing before God.

This was the reason they so violently opposed Jesus. He preached against everything they believed in and held dear. As Jesus preached the Sermon on the Mount, he explained to the crowds that formal adherence to the law was not sufficient for righteousness. He revealed the sinfulness of our hearts. Refraining from murder is a good thing, but hatred in our hearts brings judgment just the same. Avoiding sex outside of marriage is commendable, but lustfulness causes guilt as well. Repeatedly Jesus shows the weakness of the law. It reveals our sinfulness, but it is not effective in removing it from our hearts.

Here is the part that should concern some of us. Part of the reason the Pharisees opposed Jesus was because he threatened the system they so desperately depended on. They were prideful and greedy and keeping the Jewish people in bondage under the law gave them all the power. They had the nation of Israel at their feet. But that's not the only reason. They also genuinely thought they were right. In Galatians chapter one Paul is discussing his calling by God. In that description, he mentions how zealous he was for the traditions of the fathers. Paul was a zealous Pharisee prior to conversion because he genuinely thought he was right. He really felt like holding on to his conservative values and traditions was the right thing to do. The problem was, those values were the only things he and his fellow Pharisees were holding on to. They had missed the true message of the Old Testament law and they had missed the gospel.

Are you seeing the connection I'm trying to make? The Pharisees used morality and piety as a mask to cover the sinfulness of their hearts. They refused to acknowledge the wickedness in their hearts and covered it with rituals, rules, and ceremonies, and demanded others do the same. Many conservative Christians today are guilty of the same infraction. As the Pharisees overreacted to the Hellenists and made the law into something it was not, Conservative Christians have overreacted to liberalism and made Christian values into something they are not. In the process of preserving orthodoxy, they have made Christianity more about behaving properly than about the saving grace found in Christ. This is made evident in several areas of the church, the main one being our children's and student's ministries.

Results of Moralism

Children and students have been victims of the American Masquerade for decades. The church has been obsessively teaching our children how to behave, but not about the gospel. In the nineties, all a youth pastor needed to be successful was pizza, dodgeball, and purity rings. As long as the kids didn't break anything at the church and got out of high school without anyone getting a tattoo or getting pregnant it was considered a success. But, here in 2019, we see the results of this mindset. According to a LifeWay Research study, sixty-six percent of teenagers leave the church for at least a year between the ages of eighteen and twenty-two.[3] The study does not mention the number of those that eventually get back to regular church attendance, but I would venture to say it is pretty low. Those numbers were from 2017 and were actually a slight improvement from the same study done in 2007.

Why are so many teenagers leaving the church? There were five main reasons given by the study. They were moving to college, judgmental or hypocritical church members, lack of connection, church's political stance, and work responsibilities. I believe these can be reduced to two categories. The first is a lack of significance; the church is less important than work and politics, and easily forgotten during a life transition. Secondly, young people feel like they are distant from and constantly judged by the church.

These reasons can all be traced back to the message the church has been preaching for years. Behave the way we tell you to and everything will be fine. That's essentially

---

[3] Most Teenagers Drop Out of Church as Young Adults. Aaron Earls Lifeway Research.
https://lifewayresearch.com/2019/01/15/most-teenagers-drop-out-of-church-as-young-adults/   Jan. 15, 2019

the message most kids have gotten at mainstream evangelical churches over recent decades. Eventually, these kids graduate and leave their small town and go to college or move to a city and find out that the rest of the world doesn't care about mom and dad's Christian values and they can get along in life just fine without them.

This happens because our students are not being taught about the wickedness in their hearts because their parents and church leaders are masking their own sinfulness with Christian values. We haven't been teaching kids that they are hopelessly sinful and destined for an eternity in hell without Christ and our only hope is to trust in him for our salvation and dedicate ourselves to love him and follow him. We have been teaching them how to act like a Christian, but not what a Christian actually is. Purity, church attendance, tithing, abstinence, and general kindness are all good things but there is nothing about them that can save anyone. Only the gospel can give a sinner a heart of flesh and make him love Jesus and actually want to obey him, but we're missing it. We cover our shame and guilt with piety. If we tithe enough and work the food pantry enough and go to enough Bible studies, we can mask the fact we have lustful hearts and we are consumed with pride, greed, and hatred. There could not be a more accurate example of a modern-day Pharisee than the conservative Christian that has exchanged the gospel for moralism.

We Need the Gospel

Now that I have offended many of you, let's get back to the passages in Luke. Before we begin to study these texts, I want to lovingly nudge you to examine yourself. Perhaps, you should put yourself in the place of these Pharisees while reading these passages. Maybe you have placed a greater emphasis on acting like a Christian than actually trusting in Christ daily for his grace and mercy. If so, I hope the message of the gospel found in them is made real to you in a way that it never has been before. I pray that God would pour out his grace on you as we study, and the message of Jesus is made clear. That being said, let's look at these texts and find what they actually mean.

First, let's take a look at the feast in Simon's house. The "woman of the city" came into Simon's house while he was hosting a feast with Jesus as the guest. This may seem odd to us, but it was customary to allow the poor into one's house during a banquet or feast so they could partake in the leftovers of the meal. This woman is said to be a sinner. There is no explanation as to what type of sin she was involved in. It's very possible she was a prostitute, but the exact nature of her sin is not important. What is important is she obviously knew she was a sinner, and so did everyone else. This woman takes advantage of the custom of the day and enters the house, but she is not there for leftovers. She goes to Jesus and literally washed his feet with her tears, wiped them with her hair, kissed, and anointed them. I cannot picture a purer, humbler, worship experience than was displayed with this woman. The love, affection, and honor she showed our Lord is something at which I marvel.

Simon was not as impressed as I am by this woman. In fact, he's actually disgusted that Jesus would even let this woman near him. In light of our new understanding of the Pharisees though, do you wonder why Simon didn't try to help this woman? For the most part, the Pharisees genuinely thought they were right, and obeying the law to their standards was the way to good standing before God. So why didn't Simon try to help her gain this righteousness that he felt he possessed. I'm sure pride is part of it, but another part is, he had nothing left to offer. This woman was marked as a sinner. She was a social outcast. The amount of times she had been instructed by fellow Jews to straighten up and obey the law is probably innumerable. Yet her sin still persisted, and Simon had nothing left to offer. If all you have to offer is a lesson on how Christians should behave, you will never be used in converting sinners to Christ. Your family, church, and community will not ever be free from the bondage of sin if all you can offer is a harsh rebuke and an order to act right.

We must have the gospel; we must have Jesus. This woman is rebellious, just like we all are. She is apparently stubbornly prideful as well. She stuck with her sin even though it made her an outcast. She was probably not overly concerned with pleasing and serving authority figures, or she would have conceded to people like the Pharisees and their standards just to fit in. However, we see her here at the feet of Jesus washing his feet with her hair. What is the cause of this humility? What brings her to this place of pure worship and submission? It is grace. She sees in Jesus, mercy. A woman who wouldn't even obey the rules to be accepted in her own culture is now worshiping at the feet of Jesus because his grace frees us from sin. The law applies pressure from the outside, restricting and binding us. Grace changes us from the inside. We are given a new nature in Christ and obedience is now a delight. We still struggle of course, but we have a genuine desire to please our Savior. That's what this woman found in Jesus.

Her act of love did not save her, it was a result of her being saved. Jesus explains this in his parable to Simon. The debtor that was forgiven the most debt loved the moneylender more. Simon did not even show Jesus what was considered common courtesy for a guest. There was no kiss, no oil, no feet washing. His lack of love toward Jesus stemmed from a lack of forgiveness. He had no faith in Jesus so there was no forgiveness. He didn't know grace; he didn't love God. He was too busy trying to pay the moneylender back to have faith in the forgiveness of the moneylender. True converts, people who know God's grace will be compelled to serve him. Servants that love the master don't need to be whipped; they obey willingly. Does that mean that a true Christian will never need rebuke, correction, or encouragement? Of course not, we still have the flesh to contend with. The point is, true change comes when we have faith in Christ and he graciously gives us a new heart that genuinely loves him.

I believe you church leaders and parents genuinely love your children, congregants, and neighbors. I believe you try so hard to preach Christian values to them because you want them to have a happy life and be righteous in the eyes of God. So, I encourage you, the way to accomplish your goal is not through coercion. It is through teaching them the gospel. If all you have to offer is the same thing Simon had to offer, your loved ones will go on sinning just like the woman in this story. Only with Jesus is a life truly changed and a person truly made to love and be obedient to Christ.

Now to the parable of the tax collector. What we take away from these passages is similar, but there are some subtle variances. With the woman in Simon's house, we learn a valuable lesson. Jesus desires genuine affection more than cold, formal obedience. It's one thing to be obedient in church attendance and tithing, it's another to be on your face weeping with joy at the feet of the Savior. Obedience is commanded of Christians and we should obey, but it should be fueled by a love and a passion for the Redeemer that forgave us our sins. The parable of the tax collector teaches us the importance of taking off the mask of morality to attain righteousness.

The tax collector would have been considered among the most awful sinners. He was a traitor to his country, collecting taxes on behalf of the Roman oppressors from his fellow Jews. Corruption among tax collectors was not uncommon. He was, as the woman, a marked sinner. He approaches the temple and cannot even bear to draw near. All he can do is cry out for mercy. The Pharisee, however, simply praises his own piety in the form of a prayer. Jesus tells us the tax collector is the one that walked away righteous. How can that be?

A problem that occurs when people grow up in church, especially in the Bible Belt, is they often grow up thinking they are doing alright. They have not sinned as others have. They aren't degenerates like those people out on the coast or in the big cities. They have lived a generally pious life. What they fail to realize is what we have already discussed. While their behavior might be impeccable, their hearts are black with sin. They may participate in every religious activity available, but without Christ, it is all worthless. What made the tax collector righteous was his dependence upon God for mercy. He recognized the law could not save him and his only hope was God's grace and mercy. Churchgoer, if you are trusting in your own obedience for your eternity, you are in a very dangerous state. I urge you to weep over your sinfulness like the tax collector and throw yourself at the feet of Jesus like the woman of the city.

Until the church recovers the truths found in these two passages, it will continue to be ineffective. We cannot preach Christian values without preaching the gospel also. This not only applies to our preaching and teaching, but also to the way we engage the culture on certain issues. The church has decided to fight moral battles against the culture by removing the gospel and the word of God from our defense. And we wonder why we are not being effective.

Keep the Gospel Central

In the wake of the Supreme Court decision on same-sex marriage, I heard all kinds of arguments against homosexuality. One major red flag I kept seeing was Christians using extrabiblical arguments against gay marriage. What I mean by this is, Christians were condemning and arguing against same-sex marriage, but they were not using the Bible in their argument. The primary concern, it seemed, was for our society as a whole. The argument was that same-sex marriage weakened the family structure. With a weakened family structure, the nation's children will be raised in a less stable environment. Due to this less stable upbringing, those children will grow up to be less productive than they would have had they been raised in a traditional family. Our economy and society as a whole will suffer from this new generation of unproductive citizens and eventually crumble. Parts of this argument I agree with, although the crumbling of western civilization because of same-sex marriage being allowed seems like a stretch. There is one thing I completely disagree with, however. That is why it matters in the first place.

Based on this argument, the primary concern we should have is the survival of our society and economy. Those should not be our main concerns as Christians. Our main concern as Christians should be glorifying God and advancing his kingdom. I oppose same-sex marriage because the Bible teaches homosexuality to be a sin. Jesus affirms the Old Testament teaching of marriage and the family in Matthew 19 and Mark 10. Paul clearly declares homosexuality to be a sin in the epistles. I do not oppose homosexuality because it makes me uncomfortable or because I'm concerned about the survival of western civilization. I oppose it because God opposes it. When the church takes a stand on moral issues and we lean on arguments other than Scripture, we willingly give up our footing. God's word is the ultimate standard of morality and should be the basis of all our defenses against the culture.

The mainstream pro-life movement is probably the guiltiest of pushing a behavior instead of standing for God's word and the gospel. Recently, Students for Life, a branch of this mainstream movement released a list of what they referred to as "bad pro-life slogans." Included in this list were things like God hates abortion, the Bible says . . . , abortion kills children, and stop abortion now.[4] These are slogans that are considered "bad" by the mainstream pro-life movement, a supposedly Christian movement. The problem is, it's not Christian at all. Furthermore, if we remove Christianity and God's word, there is no basis for a pro-life movement. Exodus 20:13 commands us not to murder. One can read through Psalm 139 and clearly see that Scripture teaches that life begins at conception. So, taking an innocent life at any point after conception is murder. Psalm 82:3 commands us to defend those that are defenseless.

These are the reasons Christians should oppose abortion. God does hate abortion, the Bible tells us that,

[4] "Bad Pro-Life Sign Slogans" Students For Life. studentsforlife.org https://studentsforlife.org/bad-pro-life-sign-slogans/

it kills children, and it should stop now. If you remove God's word, why do we even care about abortion? What moral responsibility do we have to fight for these unborn children? Furthermore, Protestants in this movement have predominantly given the lead to the Roman Catholic church. Because of this, the gospel is not preached and has no place in the movement. The life-giving, redeeming, heart-changing message of Christ is not being given to those mothers and fathers at abortion clinics. This is why supposedly Christian movements that remove God's word and the gospel are not, and never will be, effective in achieving anything.

We should take a stand for God's word and his revealed will and character, and the gospel should be the core of our message. It must remain central. When we oppose things like homosexuality and abortion it is not to demand they meet our personal standard of morality. It is to reveal God's truth and their sinfulness to them and offer them the gospel. Hateful speech and coercion will not eliminate sin. They are image-bearers of God lost in sin. We should love them enough to offer them forgiveness in Christ. The same forgiveness we need, the same mercy we cling to. Anytime we confront sin in the culture it should be done in love. We are not called to spread hate; we are called to represent God and preach the message of his redemptive work.

Sin cannot be dealt with by simply putting on a mask of morality. Your children, your neighbors, and you need the gospel. You need to recognize your sinfulness and your need for Jesus. Stop pretending you are righteous, you're not. Take off the mask and trust in Christ and urge others to do the same.

THE UNCONVERTED CHURCH

THE MASK OF morality has had horrific effects on the church. The lack of the true gospel being preached in churches throughout the nation has led to churches full of people that don't understand the gospel and are not actually Christians. Many churchgoers don't actually know what it means to be a Christian. They are culturally Christian, but they are unconverted.

Let me take a moment to explain the difference between a cultural Christian and a converted Christian as this might be a new language to some. When I say cultural Christian, the person I am referring to is someone who is merely associated with Christianity. They are most likely a church member and attend at least semi-regularly, probably the same church their parents, grandparents, and great grandparents attended. They find a great deal of value in Christian principles and will say they believe in God and the Bible. So far so good, but, this same churchgoer that believes in God and the Bible could not articulate the gospel in an understandable manner. They know nothing of justification, atonement, or Christ's imputed righteousness. In addition to their lack of gospel, knowledge is a lack of visible spiritual fruit. While they attend church, they don't have any real commitment to the local body of believers and any minor inconvenience or opportunity for something more entertaining will keep them away from the weekly gathering. In fact, apart from their spotty church attendance and lip service to God and the Bible, it would seem that Christ has no real impact on their life at all. He is never the topic of conversation and he never gets a second thought when making major life decisions. This is the cultural Christian.

The cultural Christian population is well represented in the Bible Belt. They are plentiful in those communities where the association with a church is expected and it is advantageous to be in the Christian crowd. They go out and have a good time on Saturday night and wake up just in time to drag themselves into church on Sunday morning. Unfortunately, many pastors turn a blind eye to this and will not preach against nominalism too strongly because their numbers are in decline anyway. They cannot afford to run people off by being too harsh. So, the cultural Christian tarries on through life feeling perfectly secure in their shallow faith. After all, they're "a good 'ole boy." Why would God find any fault in them? Sure, they're not perfect, but they work hard, take care of their family, and give God his due (at least, they think they do). They are pacified by weak pastors and the nominal Christian culture around them until one day this life ends, and they find, too late, that the twenty they threw in the plate every couple of weeks was not enough to get them to heaven. This is the tragic reality for people sitting in pews all across the nation every Sunday morning. I believe Jesus' warning in Matthew 7:22 should bring a tear to the eye and send a chill down the spine of every pastor in the Bible Belt.

In contrast, the converted Christian is an individual that has been brought from death to life. Their heart of stone has been removed and they have been given a heart of flesh (Ezekiel 36:26). They have truly come to the realization that they are sinful beyond rescue, but Christ did the impossible and paid the price for their sins and gave them life and affection for God and his commands. They now love God and have an authentic desire to please him out of appreciation for his grace. Tragically, I would presume that the cultural Christians outnumber these converted Christians through the Bible Belt.

As mentioned earlier, the mask of morality has brought about the ignorance of the gospel in churches everywhere. More specifically, however, there are two areas of theology the church has become ignorant in that have played major roles in the creation of the unconverted church. The first is soteriology. This is our understanding of salvation. What does it mean to be saved? What does it mean to be a Christian? There is a lot of churchgoers that cannot answer these questions. The other area is ecclesiology. This is our understanding of the church. What is the purpose of the church? What is the specific purpose of the local church?

These questions can be, at times, hotly debated between denominations. Sadly though, it seems most professing Christians don't care to put in the effort to study the subject. Misunderstandings in salvation and the church and its function have led to local churches being made up of nominal, cultural Christians. Not only are these unbelievers pacified, but the converted Christians are also spiritually starved. We need to regain an understanding of salvation and church, so we don't sit idly by while groves of people sit sleepily in a pew until their damnation and Christians are rendered useless for the kingdom because they are not being nurtured with the biblical teaching of the gospel.

Salvation

Let us begin with a discussion of salvation. To learn what it is to be saved, we must first understand what it is to be lost. Most churchgoers know the story of the fall. In the first two chapters of Genesis, we see the account of creation. God spoke the universe and everything in it into existence. He also gave the creature that was made in his image, man, a command. He forbade Adam and Eve from the fruit from a particular tree. Genesis three records the events that followed. Adam and Eve were deceived by Satan, disobeyed God, and were removed from Eden. Not only were our first parents barred from paradise, but all of humanity was also cursed with sin. But what is this sinful state we find ourselves in? What does it mean to be sinful? Paul explains the current state of humanity in Romans 3:10-18:

"None is righteous, no not one; no one understands; no one seeks for God. All have turned aside; together they have become worthless; no one does good, not even one. Their throat is an open grave; they use their tongues to deceive. The venom of asps is under their lips. Their mouth is full of curses and bitterness. Their feet are swift to shed blood; in their paths are ruin and misery, and the way of peace they have not known. There is no fear of God before their eyes."

The description Paul gave is a description of every human apart from Christ. You might be thinking, "this is describing a psychopath, I've never been this evil or even know anyone this evil." You're right, the person Paul is describing is deceitful, murderous, and hateful toward God. The person he is describing, like it or not, is you. How can that be? You don't shed blood or leave ruin and misery in your wake. You may not, but you would if you were allowed to. Paul is describing what is in the deepest part of everyone's heart. Thankfully, God doesn't allow most people to go to those depths. In Romans 1:24 Paul says, "God gave them up in the lusts of their hearts" and in 1:26 he says, "God gave them up to dishonorable passions." For God to give people over to their sin, there had to be some sort of restraint, to begin with. God, in His grace, does not allow most people to reach the depths of their depravity. So no, you may not be as bad as the description given in Romans 3, at least on the outside. The truth remains, however, your heart is absolutely wicked to the core. That is what is meant by a person being lost in sin.

The kind of wickedness and rebellion that resides in our hearts makes us worthy of hell. The consequences of sin are reaffirmed in Romans 6:23, the result of disobeying God is death. The sinfulness inherent within each of us causes us to be born with an inclination toward disobedience. We naturally rebel and offend the holy God, the Creator of the universe. Therefore, our nature condemns us. From birth, we are worthy of eternal punishment and have no way of attaining the righteousness needed to be in good standing with God because of our inherent sinful nature.

There is hope for humanity, however. In Genesis 3:15, during God's pronouncement of judgment upon Adam and Eve, he promises a Redeemer. God vows to one day provide a rescue from sin. Our Rescuer is Jesus Christ. "For while we were still weak, at the right time Christ died for the ungodly . . . God shows his love for us in that while we were still sinners, Christ died for us. Since therefore, we have been justified by his blood, much more shall we be saved by him from the wrath of God." (Romans 5:6-9) Christ took the punishment for his people. He was innocent but willingly suffered so we wouldn't have to. He also provided us with righteousness. We are not righteous; he gives us his righteousness. This is the gospel. Jesus took our place under the Father's wrath and gave us good standing before the Father.

This atonement for our sins and Christ's righteousness are made available to us through faith. Ephesians 2:8 tells us that salvation is the product of God's grace and it is given to us through faith. What this means is our salvation, graciously given by God, is applied to us through faith. Our trust and belief in Christ are the means through which salvation is given, and the evidence that confirms it because "no one can say 'Jesus is Lord' except by the Spirit." (1 Corinthians 12:3) When salvation is applied through faith, regeneration comes with it. Ezekiel 36:26 describes it as having our hearts of stone removed and replaced with hearts of flesh. That hateful, wicked nature from Romans 3 that controls us is overthrown. We are brought from death to life. The new creation now has a desire to please God and therefore, repents of their sin and commits to follow Jesus Christ faithfully. This love for God and commitment to him are not the means of salvation but the result of it.

After this conversion. After a person believes in Christ, is given a new heart, and clings to the cross of

Christ, they enter into a process called sanctification. Romans 8:28-29 is misused more than, possibly, any other piece of Scripture besides Jeremiah 29:11. Many believe these verses teach that God just ultimately wants what's best for you. Of course, "best for you" is typically defined by what we think is best and not God. What these verses actually teach is that, for the believer, God works through the Spirit to use everything in their life to gradually conform them to the image of Christ. This transforming process begins at conversion and continues until death.

So, we should understand that the converted Christians will have an awareness of their sinfulness and need for a Savior. They will trust in Christ as that Savior and have a desire to please him out of appreciation for his grace and mercy. There will also be evidence of a transformational process taking place within them in which they are becoming more like Christ. That is not to say they are made instantly perfect; it is simply to say there is evidence of some change continually taking place conforming them to the image of Christ. Does this describe you?

Perhaps you were scoffing at the idea of the cultural Christian earlier in this chapter but now realize there is no evidence you are actually converted. I'm not writing this to cause doubt; I'm writing it to cause you to examine yourself. I don't want you to be one of those cultural Christians walking blindly into eternal judgment. If you have come to the realization that this converted Christian does not describe you, stop reading, pray that God would break your heart over your sin, and bring you to faith in Christ. I hope and pray that everyone who reads this book will be a born again, converted Christian and I will get to enjoy eternity in Christ with you.

The Church

Now that we've studied soteriology, it's possible that you have begun to not only examine yourself but also consider the eternal security of those you spend every Sunday with at church. Maybe now you too are seeing what I am seeing. Perhaps you're beginning to think, "if that is what a converted Christian is, there are a lot of unconverted people in the church." And maybe that would prompt you to wonder how that could happen. How could a local church, surrounded by Christian things and the Bible, be full of non-Christians? Part of the answer is the teaching of moralism as opposed to the gospel as discussed in the last chapter. The other part is the church has lost its purpose. We don't know what the local church is supposed to do anymore.

We must first make two things clear. The church consists of all true Christians, past and present. This is the universal church. These are the people we will spend eternity with and there are certain obligations we have to the church. There is also the local assembly of believers. This is a gathering of believers in a local setting. Your church that you attend each week is the local assembly of believers. Our understanding of this local assembly and what it should do has been skewed over the last few decades and this has led to the unconverted church.

If you ask various people what the purpose of the local church is there would undoubtedly be varied answers. Most of those answers would probably be technically correct, as the local church has many functions, but the primary purpose of the church most likely won't be mentioned. Jonathon Leeman gives a clear and concise answer to the question, "the local church is the authority on earth that Jesus has instituted to officially affirm and give shape to my Christian life and yours."[5] That may be an offensive definition for many, but it is true. If you claim to be a Christian and therefore represent Christ, the local church has the authority to affirm or deny your claim, and to oversee your growth in sanctification.

How can you say something like that? My relationship with Jesus is personal. No one has a right to affirm or deny me. I don't need anyone to oversee me. I understand this might be the reaction of a few readers, but I assure you, Leeman's definition is very biblical. We see this authority given in Matthew 16:18-19:

"And I tell you, you are Peter, and on this rock, I will build my church, and the gates of hell shall not prevail against it. I will give you the keys of the kingdom of heaven and whatever you bind on earth shall be bound in heaven, and whatever you loose on earth shall be loosed in heaven."

This has been a hotly debated passage. The Roman Catholics use it to justify the office of the pope. They believe Jesus is establishing the office in what he says to Peter. That is a misunderstanding, however. The idea that

---

[5] Leeman, Jonathon. Church Membership: How the World Knows Who Represents Jesus. Crossway. Wheaton Illinois. 2012 (pg 24)

Peter was given more authority than the other apostles is not well supported. In fact, in Galatians 2:11-14, Paul opposes and corrects him. If Peter had some sort of special authority or infallibility it is hard to imagine Paul being so bold to confront and correct his behavior. Also, in Acts 15, during the Jerusalem council, it would seem that James is the authoritative figure of the council rather than Peter. The idea that special authority was given and the office of pope instituted simply cannot be supported.

What Jesus was referring to was not Peter personally, but his confession. Peter had just confessed Jesus to be the Messiah. Christ's church is built on the gospel. It is founded on the truth of his incarnation, death, and resurrection. Affirming the gospel and confessing Jesus as Lord and Savior is what makes someone a part of the church. The rock Jesus is referring to is the truth of the gospel. It is through the church that Jesus will advance his kingdom and hell will not be able to stop our advance. We see this at the ascension in Matthew 28 as he charges us with carrying out this purpose and instructs us to use the gospel as our weapon as we advance.

Jesus also gives the keys of the kingdom to Peter and gives him the authority to bind and loose. Again, this is not establishing the papacy. This authority is also granted to the other apostles as they would make the same confession Peter did, and to all those that would come after them. The giving of the keys represents the giving of the gospel message. The way into the kingdom is the gospel. We invite people in when we preach the gospel to them. Possessing the key also makes the church a type of gatekeeper. This is where the binding and loosing comes in. It is the responsibility of the church as a whole, not the individual, to affirm or deny a person's confession. The church decides who is recognized as a member of the kingdom, and who is not. And once a person is affirmed, the church oversees them. Being a part of a local church means submitting to the authority of that church and being corrected if needed.

If the problem of the unconverted church is going to be dealt with, we have to start with soteriology and ecclesiology. We have to know what it means to be saved and to be a Christian. We also have to know what the primary function and purpose of the church is. We have to know the difference between a converted Christian and a cultural Christian. We also have to have church structures that don't allow cultural Christians to wander blindly through life with a false sense of assurance. We need to preach the pure gospel. Stop worrying about offending people and preach the truth. Our churches need to be structured in a way that requires some kind of commitment or membership to be considered a part of the local body. There should be a process in place that enables the church to affirm or deny an individual's confession and reject or accept their membership request. Church discipline must also be a function of the local church. The specific structures will vary depending on the denomination you are a part of, but these elements must be present if the church is going to serve its true purpose, and not be an accomplice in the false assurance of nominal Christians.

THE NATION HAS BECOME GOD

IN CHAPTER ONE we studied the Pharisees. We learned that while they are the most hated characters in the New Testament, their beginnings were actually quite pure and noble. They wanted to see their nation get back to the traditions and values they had once held so dearly. However, over time they had drifted into idolatry. In the first chapter we primarily discussed their idolatry of the law, but that was not the only thing they idolized. They also idolized the nation of Israel itself. This was a big reason for their opposition to Jesus.

For many 1st century Jews, the Messiah was thought to be a political savior promised to the nation of Israel. This is why the disciples had such a difficult time understanding Jesus' teaching. When we talked about the church, we examined the exchange between Jesus and Peter in Matthew 16. If you continue on from that passage to 16:21-23 you will see that while Peter rightly confessed Jesus to be the Messiah, he still did not fully

47

understand the purpose of the Messiah's coming. The idea of the Messiah suffering, and especially dying, did not fit the common Jewish expectation of the Messiah. They expected him to lead a political uprising and overthrow the Roman Empire, returning the nation of Israel to the splendor of past days under the reign of David and Solomon. It would not be until after the resurrection that the disciples would fully realize what Jesus was actually on earth to accomplish.

Many of the Pharisees would never come to a true knowledge of Jesus or the gospel message, even after the resurrection. Their misunderstanding of the Messiah blinded their judgment. The Pharisees and other religious leader's misunderstanding of the Messiah are actually what led to the crucifixion of Jesus. They were expecting a political leader that would rescue the nation from the oppression of Rome, but Jesus was quite the opposite of that. He spoke of judgment for Israel, not restoration. In Luke 21:5-6 Jesus predicts the destruction of the temple and in Luke 21:20-24, he describes the destruction of the entire city of Jerusalem.

Imagine, if you will, an individual that was going around predicting the destruction of Washington D.C. He was telling everyone of a time in which the White

House, Capitol Building, and every other government building there would be torn completely down and burned. I would imagine this would bring some amount of horror to you, especially if you believed it could actually happen. To the 1st century Jew, Jesus' prediction of the destruction of the temple and Jerusalem would have been equal to that feeling of shock and fear, or most likely even greater. In the mind of a Pharisee, there was no way Jesus could be the Messiah if he's saying things like this. Therefore, his claim to be the Messiah must be false, and so they crucified him. Their misunderstanding of the Messiah and love for their nation led them to kill God in the flesh.

Where the Pharisees and many of the Jewish people went wrong was, they had begun to believe the nation of Israel was an end in itself. They felt as though the nation was essential to God's glory and work. If the nation fell, God lost. In their minds, the success of the nation was the only way God could reveal his power and sovereignty to the world. Paul sheds some light on Israel's real purpose for us in Galatians 3:7-14:

"Know then that it is those of faith who are the sons of Abraham. And the Scripture, foreseeing that God would justify the Gentiles by faith, preached the gospel beforehand to Abraham saying, 'In you shall all the nations be blessed.' So then, those who are of faith are blessed along with Abraham, the man of faith . . . Christ redeemed us from the curse of the law . . . so that in Christ Jesus the blessing of Abraham might come to the Gentiles so that we might receive the promised Spirit through faith."

God created a nation through Abraham, the nation of Israel, for the purpose of giving a blessing to the rest of the world through that nation. The blessing is Jesus Christ and his redemption. The purpose of Israel was to be a part of God's plan of redemption. We were given the law through the nation of Israel so we would know what sin is. We were given the temple and the sacrifices so we would understand the atonement. Finally, through the nation of Israel, came Jesus. He is the ultimate atonement for our sins, and he was given by God to the world through Israel. The Pharisees, being conservative nationalists, missed the bigger picture of God's redemptive work and wanted Israel to be the center of God's work. They did not like the idea of their nation as only a part of God's plan, a mere tool. They believed God's authority and power to rise and fall with their nation.

The American Pharisee

When we discussed the mask of morality, I gently nudged you to examine yourself. I wanted you to ask yourself if, perhaps, you had become a Pharisee in some way. I ask the same thing of you here as well. There are a great number of professing Christians in the American church that have lost sight of the bigger picture of God's redemptive work because they have made an idol out of our nation.

Many American Christians believe the United States to be a modern-day Israel. As the Israelites were oppressed in Egypt, true Christians were oppressed in Europe under the rule of false churches. They made their exodus and came to a new land to establish a nation that would be true to God and his teachings. Instead of the Red Sea, our founders were led across the Atlantic. The oppressive king of England kept them under his thumb in the new land for a time, but the American spirit led to a revolution and the early Americans eventually shook off all the chains of their bondage. They were now free to begin building a nation that would truly be God's and carry out his purposes. We carried out our purpose as God's new chosen nation well until the recent liberal movement deceived and corrupted our children. Does this describe your view of the United States? This understanding of our country is what has caused many to idolize it over God.

There are some issues that arise from a view such as this. The first arises with the early Americans. The general assumption by many conservatives is that our nation was founded by devout Christians that were committed to creating a nation with the sole purpose of serving and glorifying God. That is not quite true. Yes, many of the colonists and founders were devout Christians. They came to America simply to escape persecution and worship God, but this does not describe all the early Americans. Different forms of deism were very popular during this time period. Deism, essentially, is the belief that the world was created by some higher being, but this being is now distant and does not interact personally with its creation. Benjamin Franklin, Thomas Jefferson, and John Adams are just a few of our founders that adhered to deism. Again, many early Americans were devout Christians, and many founders were influenced greatly by Christianity in building the nation, but to say that the founding of our nation was strictly Christian would simply be incorrect. Religious freedom was important, as were all freedoms, but it was not specifically Christian.

Another characteristic I see in conservatives that isn't quite accurate is, they always believe the "old days" were better. The average conservative is generally obsessed with getting back to the way things used to be because they were obviously better. I can imagine a 1st century Pharisee doing the same thing. I'm sure they would read about the times of David and Solomon and how fruitful the nation was and long to get back to that. I'm sure they remembered their childhood and would say things like, "I remember the good old days before these Hellenists (promoters of Greek culture a.k.a. liberals) took over." Compare this to the modern American conservative. We long for the old days when times were simpler. We want Mayberry and Green Acres back. We want to get back to when this nation had morals and stood for something.

It is interesting what nostalgia does to us. We always look back and see times past as much better than they really were. Was our morality really that much purer in the old days? I would ask the Pharisee the same thing. David was a good king for a while. But after a time, he committed adultery and murder. Later, the royal family was torn apart and murderous toward one another and

David had to flee for his life from his son. His successor, Solomon, ventured into areas of immorality many of us cannot imagine. He indulged in every lust that arose within him and the nation suffered morally because of it. Just before Jesus' time on earth, there was a conservative resurgence in Israel and they even won their independence as a nation for a short time. But that time was marked by high priests being installed through assassinations and coercion and the entire religious structure was corrupted beyond repair. Is that really the good old days you want to go back to? Is that your idea of a perfect society?

Now let's turn that question back to the American conservative. In the 1860's we had a large group of the population that was willing to kill and be killed in order to maintain their legal right to own another human being. I know a good southerner will say the Civil War was a war of state's rights against a centralized government but, if we are honest, it doesn't take much study to realize the primary issue was slavery. The Southern Baptist Convention was created because even Christians wanted to keep slaves.

Move along to the early 1900s and alcoholism is so rampant that an extreme prohibition movement was able to amend the constitution banning alcohol. Instead of this amendment helping, crime and corruption grew so bad we are still making movies about it today. Move on to the golden years of the '50s and '60s and we have massive civil unrest over the Vietnam War, systemic racism, and the beginning of the sexual revolution. I could go on, but you get my point. What are you trying to go back to? At what point was the United States of America a beacon of perfect morality?

I am in no way trying to run down this great nation. Despite all our flaws, I would not want to live anywhere else. The freedom we have within our borders is unmatched and the American spirit and ingenuity is something to marvel at. I thank God for our nation and the opportunity to live here and be a citizen. I simply do not want to make this nation into something it is not. I don't want to make it into a god. Which, I am afraid, is what many conservatives have done.

The Effects of Idolatry

Because many conservatives view the United States as a modern-day Israel, they have fallen into the same trap the Pharisees did. They have begun to believe God needs the United States. They consider us the strong tower of

Christianity in the world. They believe God's glory rises and falls with us. If we lose, he loses. This is simply not the case. Even if we were a chosen nation, we would only be a tool used by God, not essential to his success as we saw in our study of the nation of Israel. God does not need a nation to call his own. He already has a people.

If you are a Christian, you are "a chosen race, a royal priesthood, a holy nation, a people for his own possession, that you may proclaim the excellencies of him who called you out of darkness into his marvelous light. Once you were not a people, but now you are God's people; once you had not received mercy, but now you have received mercy." (1 Peter 2:9-10) God works through his church to advance his kingdom. The church is global. We do not have the market cornered on Christianity. God does not need the United States of America for anything. Our idolatry of the nation has led to many problems, but there are three that I believe are the most prevalent.

The first is, many American religious conservatives believe "American" to be synonymous with "Christian." We truly do believe to be a good American is to be a good Christian, and to be a good Christian is to be a good American. If you don't believe me just get on YouTube and watch some 4th of July services at FBC Dallas. It is difficult to tell who or what is being worshiped, God, or the nation. For many, the nation has replaced God. This is evident in many of the mottos that conservatives have taken to. "I stand for the flag and kneel for the cross" is one of the most popular. If you want to stand during the pledge or the national anthem to show respect for your country, I respect you for that. But, don't place showing respect for your country and bowing before the Redeemer of humanity on the same level. All you're doing is trivializing the gospel. You are telling the world that the flag of our nation is just as important as the cross of Christ. That flag is not the place in which Jesus Christ was tortured and suffered the wrath of the Father so his people could have eternal life. That flag did not hold up the Lamb of God in shame and despair as his own people mocked him. That flag does not hold the power to make a sinful, wretched human being to be in good standing before the God of the universe. Stand and/or kneel for whatever you like, but never think that the flag of any nation holds the same significance that the cross of Jesus Christ does.

Americanized Christianity is so strong that it even shapes most American's views of the Bible. Eschatology is the study of end times. I'm sure most people that grew up in church and are between the ages of 25-50 have read or watched Left Behind. Left Behind is a dramatic portrayal of what is referred to as premillennial dispensationalism. Now, I am not going to get into a discussion on end times in this book. I am only mentioning this to further explain my point. Premillennial dispensationalism has only been around for about 150 years and it is primarily an American view. What has happened is, we as Americans are so arrogant and self-centered that we have rejected almost two thousand years of teachings on eschatology. We have done this because the Left Behind type of eschatology allows the United States an opportunity to be included in the prophecies of the book of Revelation. Do you see what has happened? We, as Americans, believe our nation to be so important and significant that we could not imagine some part of Scripture not including us. So, we simply turned a blind eye to historic teaching on the end times and looked to a system that reads us into the Bible. We have to realize that the United States is not at the center of everything and God does not need us to complete his plans.

The second problem brought on by idolizing the nation is a moral compromise. In the 1st century, the Pharisees really only had two things on their mind. They were concerned with preserving the nation and eventually restoring it. They wanted to do what they could to at least maintain the status quo of the culture and not see the nation wiped out. They also wanted to eventually see the nation restored to how they were in the good old days. They would do anything if they supported these two causes. They became so narrow-minded in this that they missed the bigger picture of God's redemptive plan. They were also greatly compromised in areas of morality. Being under the rule of the Roman Empire, it was critical for Israel to maintain a good relationship with Rome. The Romans were not pleasant people to deal with and if you got out of line too badly, they would just wipe you off the map. In fact, in A.D. 70, that's exactly what they did to the nation of Israel. The leaders of Israel knew about Rome's brutality, so they compromised a great deal to stay in good graces with the Roman officials.

The greatest compromise, however, was the murder of Jesus. Remember, Jesus was viewed as a threat to their cause. They wanted the nation restored; he spoke of its destruction. So, because of their idolatry of the nation, they committed murder. They held court at night, which is a violation of the law. They paid witnesses to lie. They manipulated Pilate, and finally, they murdered an innocent man simply because he, they thought, posed a threat to the nation. Their idolatry of the nation of Israel led them to murder the Son of God.

I have noticed this same kind of moral compromise in American Christians today. I'm not accusing Christians of being lying murderers. I would just like to point out that many professing Christians have compromised a great deal for the sake of the nation. One way in which this compromise has shown itself is with our President. I know some of you probably cussed when I mentioned Donald Trump is considered by some a moral degenerate in the introduction, and you're not going to like what I have to say next, but please hear me out. I don't like or dislike Mr. Trump enough to satisfy either side, we should make that clear now. This is not about his presidency or arguing over his policies. This is about the church's reaction to him.

I believe James 4:12 instructs us to refrain from making definitive judgments about another person's salvation as individuals. So, I will not say that there is no way Mr. Trump is a Christian. However, we can be discerning and examine the evidence of people's fruit and their confession. If you'll remember from the previous chapter, we actually should make these kinds of judgments before allowing a professing Christian into our local church as a member. All I will say is, if Donald Trump were in an interview at my church with the lead pastor and me, I doubt we would feel confident enough in his confession to allow him into membership. I have heard him say things about God, but nothing of the gospel and his morality is questionable at best. There does not appear to be any kind of real repentance or transformation taking place. I would hope that the sincere, discerning Christian can see what I have just explained and, even if reluctantly, agree with me.

Now that we have gotten that out of the way, it is time to get to the point. We have a most-likely, non-Christian individual with questionable morals as President of the United States, and the religious conservatives have absolutely fallen in love with him. There are leading figures in the church that make him out to be God's chosen man. He is considered the savior of western civilization. I believe in God's sovereignty; therefore, I do believe God wanted Mr. Trump to win the election or he wouldn't have. But, for the church to champion, this man as a pillar of morality and the one to lead us back to a pure and God-honoring culture seems a bit odd. Why would religious conservatives so fully support such a man?

It's actually quite simple. They support Mr. Trump for the same reason the Pharisees killed Jesus, to protect the nation. American conservatives want the same things the Pharisees did. They want to preserve the nation and prevent it from crumbling. Then their ultimate goal is to bring it back to the image of times past they keep in their head. Hillary Clinton and the Democrats were threatening to take those things away from them, and Mr. Trump was simultaneously offering them those very things, so the conservatives whole-heartedly supported a man that is probably not a Christian and is, I'll just say it, a moral degenerate. This is just another symptom of the idolatry of the nation. We compromise because we are more concerned about the welfare of the nation than about God's purpose.

The third result of idolizing the nation is the politicizing of the church. Christian is just another word for Republican to many. We have become nothing more than religious right-wingers, and politicians know this. Christians have been manipulated over and over by politicians to get votes and we are not able to see it. I mentioned the mainstream pro-life movement in the first chapter. That movement is just a political machine built to get votes from Christians. They have done virtually nothing to actually stop abortion. They really don't want it to end because then they would not have a platform. Christians have become mere pawns in the politician's chess game, and we have done it to ourselves.

We have come to this because we have made everything about politics. Because we idolize our ideas of the nation so badly, we rely on politicians. Instead of the Christians actually leaving their homes and churches and engaging the culture, we would rather vote for politicians that will force the culture to behave the way we like through legislation. This mindset has come back to bite us. The system has turned on us and we are the ones being legislated out. The church has to stop trying to rely on the political system. The idol you have served has turned on you. Fight for things on a moral basis, not political. Take a stand for God's truth, not a political platform. Be a Christian, not a Republican.

As this chapter comes to an end, let me leave you with something to consider. The idolization of the nation is really the result of a battle between two identities. Do you identify as an American, or a Christian? As Christians, we are a people that God has called to himself. We have a higher purpose than that of any nation. We are a part of God's kingdom. We are heirs with Christ. We are entrusted with the life-saving message of Christ. You can love your country, but your identity should be in Christ alone. I don't want you to miss out on God's redemptive plan because you can't see past the borders of the United States.

SUFFERING ISN'T WHAT IT USED TO BE

WHILE THE EARLY Christians would marvel at the idolatry of the nation many American Christians are practicing, they would marvel even more at the American Christian aversion to suffering. Throughout history there have been times in which Christianity was the cultural norm and persecution was nonexistent, but never to the extent and the duration the western church has experienced. This long span of cultural dominance has led to the state we now find ourselves in. Many professing Christians are really just holding to a set of values and know nothing of the true gospel. Also, the idea of suffering as a direct result of our faith shakes us to our very core.

You're Not Being Persecuted

I know there will be someone out there that will disagree with this chapter because they feel as though they are being persecuted. Trust me, you're not. I will admit that it does appear as though the cultural dominance of Christianity is rapidly fading, I'll talk about why that's a good thing in a minute, but you are not "suffering" for Christ. If you want to know suffering, study the early church.

Early Christians experienced waves of persecution that should have wiped it out. God's sovereignty and the power of the gospel of Jesus Christ can be the only reasons for its survival. Every few years an emperor would come into power in Rome with a desire to restore the empire to its past glory. Several of these emperors were convinced the only way to do that would be to appease the pagan gods of their forefathers. For the most part, subjects could worship as they pleased as long as their ultimate allegiance was to the emperor and the leading pagan god. I hope you can see why this was a problem for the Christians. The first commandment is "You shall have no other gods before me." (Exodus 20:3) A Christian cannot pledge their ultimate allegiance to a false god and worship the one true God only if it is in submission to the emperor. That would be placing the emperor and his pagan gods over the only true God. Our Creator is the only being worthy of worship and praise. He is the beginning and the end. He is above all creation. So, the Christians could not do what had been commanded by their emperor.

The result of their obstinance was intense persecution. At various times they were barred from government and military jobs. They had their homes destroyed and meeting places torn down. They were arrested and tortured. They were thrown into the colosseum to be killed or just outright murdered in the streets. For about three centuries, every generation of Christians experienced a time period of some degree of persecution from the Roman Empire.

This persecution experienced by the early church is still being endured by some Christians today. Just the other day, I saw pictures of church buildings being torn down in China and South America. Christians in the Middle East are often killed for their faith in Christ and parts of India are no safer. We have brothers and sisters in Christ all over the world that are exiled from their families, lose their jobs, get blown up during church services, and are killed because they refuse to denounce their faith in Jesus Christ.

Americans are not suffering for Christ. Just because someone said something mean and anti-Christian to you on Facebook does not mean you are suffering for Christ. Just because the public-school system isn't strictly Christian and teaching your child about the Bible so you can continue to be a lazy parent does not mean that you are suffering for Christ. Yes, there are some isolated instances in which people have lost their jobs and been sued for standing up for Christian values. Yes, there have been instances of people getting arrested standing outside abortion clinics giving a voice to the unborn. Yes, there are some instances of persecution and people suffering for Christ, but if you are using these instances to prove that you do not have an aversion to suffering, you are fooling only yourself. For the overwhelming majority of Americans, especially in conservative areas, identifying with Christianity is either widely accepted or even advantageous for your social standing. Because of our mostly Christian culture, we have little or no concept of suffering as a direct result of our faith and even try to avoid it at all costs, which has not always been the case for Christians.

As Christ Suffered, So Will We

When we talk about suffering, we have to start with the suffering of Christ. Christ's mission on earth culminated in the crucifixion. His suffering was central to the plan of redemption, "Yet it was the will of the Lord to crush him; he has put him to grief; when his soul makes an offering for guilt, he shall prosper in his hand. Out of the anguish of his soul he shall see and be satisfied; by his knowledge shall the righteous one, my servant, make many to be accounted righteous, and he shall bear their iniquities." (Isaiah 53:10-11) The purpose of the incarnation was for Christ to suffer. We are made righteous before God because Christ suffered.

This model of suffering was intended to be followed by those that claim to be Christ's disciples. Jesus explains that it would be natural for there to be some friction between the world and the believer, "If the world hates you, know that it has hated me before it hated you." (John 15:18) If the world found Christ's message offensive and persecuted him because of it, it would be logical for the world to persecute those that follow and stand for that same message. In John 16:33, Jesus speaks of trouble for the Christian as if it is a basic reality and offers encouragement, "In the world, you will have tribulation, but take heart; I have overcome the world." Finally, Jesus goes so far as to imply that if you are not experiencing some burden of suffering, you are not following him, "If anyone would come after me, let him deny himself and take up his cross daily and follow me." (Luke 9:23) If we are truly going to follow Jesus, there will be some aspect of burden and suffering as a direct result of our faithfulness to Him.

The apostles seemed to understand suffering as not just a part of Christian living, but essential to it. Peter wrote, "And after you have suffered a little while, the God of all grace, who has called you to his eternal glory in Christ, will himself restore, confirm, strengthen, and establish you." (1 Peter 5:10) Paul says in 2 Corinthians 4:17 that, "For this light and momentary affliction is preparing for us an eternal weight of glory . . ." It would appear that the apostles viewed suffering as integral to the Christian life and inseparable from a true commitment to Christ. Paul makes this point clear in 2 Timothy 3:12, "Indeed, all who desire to live a godly life in Christ Jesus will be persecuted."

Not only did the apostles teach this, but they also lived it. The book of Acts records a great deal of the apostles and other early Christians' sufferings. All of the apostles were martyred with the exception of John. John, according to tradition, survived being thrown in boiling oil and his reward was being exiled until the last few years of his life. The apostles were persecuted, and they suffered, but they did not waiver and even welcomed the suffering so they could prove their faith and share in Christ's suffering. "But rejoice insofar as you share Christ's sufferings that you may also rejoice and be glad when his glory is revealed." (1 Peter 4:13) They believed their suffering in Christ now was worth being glorified in Christ upon his return.

This commitment to suffering did not end with the apostles. The accounts of early Christians willingly and voluntarily offering themselves up to the Romans will blow your mind. Martyrdom was considered an honor, and suffering was an opportunity to work out your faith. The early monastic movement was even partially a reaction to the new lack of persecution. In 324 A.D. Constantine made Christianity the legal religion of the Roman Empire. This put an end to an era of persecution for Christians. Monks began to move out into the desert to live in caves and devote themselves to God and his word. They did this for two reasons. One was the corruption and division that occurred in the church after it was made the state religion (we'll get into that a little deeper in a moment), the other reason was to suffer.

With no opportunity for martyrdom and the lack of persecution at the hands of the Romans, the monks felt they had no way to prove their faith. They felt the only thing to do to prove their devotion was to submit themselves to the harshest living conditions and strictest diets they could. Now, I am not suggesting you become a monk and live in a cave. The logic of the monks was, I believe, flawed. The idea of asceticism being required for proper Christian living is false. What I want you to focus on is the importance of suffering. Jesus, the apostles, and the early church all placed a great deal of importance on suffering. You don't have to go looking for an opportunity to be martyred, but you should have a biblical understanding of suffering and welcome it when it comes. Christ suffered for us and we will suffer to some degree if we are truly following him.

Why Do We Avoid Suffering?

The American view of suffering is far from that of Christians in centuries past. Even the possibility of mild persecution causes panic and hysteria for many Christians. In 2015, as a new pastor, I joined a group of other pastors that would meet regularly. As a young pastor, the opportunity to fellowship and visit with older, experienced ministers was a great benefit to me. I mostly enjoyed those meetings, but I noticed something when the topic of the recent Supreme Court ruling would come up in conversation. There was a certain level of fear among those seasoned pastors when it came to the implications of the ruling on same-sex marriage. It seemed most churches almost went into complete panic mode and were bringing in lawyers and doing everything they could to protect themselves from this new ruling. Now, a local church taking measures to protect itself legally is wise. I'm not suggesting we should be ignorant and foolish. It was the attitude that I found so concerning. Even my church members got caught up in it. They just knew that the government and LGBT movement were going to attack us full force and that would be the end of the church. It seemed that this fear gripped the majority of conservative Christians all over the country.

The primary fear was that the new ruling would be used to force conservative pastors and churches to officiate and host same-sex marriages or face the consequences of a lawsuit resulting in the demise of the church. First of all, this fear was blown out of proportion. While same-sex couples are obviously in rebellion against God and his word, they have greater concerns than trying to tear down churches. They are image-bearers of God lost in sin. They are not savage beasts awaiting the opportunity to rip apart any Christian or Christian institution they come across. Perhaps, if we actually viewed them as image-bearers of God in need of the same grace we are, we would have more success in reaching the LGBT community with the gospel.

The second issue with this fear is, are you really that afraid of potentially being in a legal battle as a result of taking a stand for God's truth? Peter faced execution and his only request was that he be crucified upside down because he was not worthy to have the same method of execution as Christ. Early Christians marched toward the colosseum without resistance knowing they were about to be torn apart by wild beasts for entertainment. Christians in Northern Africa sit quietly as their beheadings are filmed. Yet, we fall into a panic at the thought of a potential legal battle. We are not even willing to go to the courtroom for Christ, much less the cross or the colosseum. We avoid suffering and to some degree outright refuse to suffer for Christ. The Supreme Court ruling on same-sex marriage and the aftermath of it proved that most conservative Christians, even pastors, have a severe aversion to persecution and suffering. The question is, why?

What is the difference between the modern American Christian and the early Christians or the Christians laying down their lives in other countries today? There are probably several reasons, but two come to the surface. The first is the presence of the prosperity gospel and its infiltration into conservative churches. The prosperity gospel essentially teaches that following Jesus will bring you, you guessed it, prosperity. If you want health, follow Jesus. If you want money, follow Jesus. If you want popularity, follow Jesus. This teaching has plagued the American church for almost a century. The prosperity gospel views Jesus as a means to obtain what we want. It ignores the biblical and historical emphasis on suffering. Suffering is viewed as a sign of lacking faith and wrongdoing on the part of the one suffering.

This mindset has crept into a lot of conservative churches in some form. Even some churches that have a solid grasp of soteriology have problems with the prosperity gospel. They hold to accurate beliefs about salvation and they would never view Jesus as simply a way to get what they want, but their view of the Christian life reveals that there is a thread of the prosperity mindset in their thinking. This can be easily seen in many evangelicals' understanding of tithing. Many of them will say, "you can't out-give God." This statement is true, but the understanding, generally, is that if you give obediently, God will give you back even more. So, the person that gives faithfully will prosper financially and the person that does not give faithfully will struggle financially.

Honestly, I don't know how mere experience and observation have not stamped out this idea, but it still persists. This idea is also applied to virtually all other areas of obedience. The general understanding is, after you become a Christian, the circumstances you find yourself in are a direct result of your obedience or lack thereof. There is no room for suffering to be used by God to produce something good. If something bad has happened to you it is because you have been unfaithful. So, there are churches that are seemingly orthodox but are essentially preaching the prosperity gospel when they teach on Christian living.

This subtle, mostly unnoticed, infiltration of the prosperity gospel into otherwise orthodox churches has warped many Christians' thoughts about suffering. Suffering can only be bad. On the surface, we may say we understand that suffering is a part of following Jesus, but deep down many American Christians really don't believe a good faithful Christian should or would be made to suffer. They think suffering can only be bad and never used by God. Therefore, we should avoid suffering at all costs.

The second reason many American Christians avoid suffering is because of our ignorance of the true gospel and its hope. The reason Paul was able to call his suffering "light and momentary" is because his focus was on the future. We have misplaced our hope. The luxury and comfort we experience as a nation have caused us to become too attached to this world and place more hope in it than in eternity. And yes, if you are fully clothed and fed and had enough money to buy this book, you are living in luxury and comfort compared to the rest of the world. American Christians have lost a proper perspective of our life here on earth. We failed to understand Paul when he says, "So we do not lose heart. Though our outer self is wasting away, our inner self is being renewed day by day. For this light momentary affliction is preparing for us an eternal weight of glory beyond all comparison, as we look not to the things that are seen but to the things that are unseen. For the things that are seen are transient, but the things that are unseen are eternal." (2 Corinthians 4:16-18)

Our hope in Christ is a hope in things to come. We hope for the day when all rulers and authorities are subjected under his feet. We hope for a day when we are resurrected as he was resurrected. We hope for eternity; that is the hope of the gospel. Too many American Christians have made Christianity about hope in this world. The glory that awaits us is not a reality to them. Therefore, because this world is what they cling to, suffering takes away their hope. If this life is where our hope is, negative circumstances rob us of our hope. The American church desperately needs to rediscover the source of hope. As Christians, we hope in Christ's return, and any suffering we might experience here is only temporary and does not compare to the glory that awaits us in Christ

Suffering is Actually Good

Suffering is actually good. I know to the ears of an American Christian, that statement makes no sense, but it's true. Suffering is given to us by God, and it is actually good. God uses suffering to shape us and mold us. Our suffering is a part of the process of sanctification.

"And we know that for those who love God all things work together for good, for those who are called according to his purpose. For those who he foreknew, he also predestined to be conformed to the image of his Son, in order that he might be the firstborn among many brothers. And those whom he predestined he also called, and those whom he called he also justified, and those whom he justified he also glorified." (Romans 8:28-30)

The Christian life begins when we are called and justified. We trust in Christ and confess him as Lord and Savior. The next step is sanctification in which we are gradually transformed into the image of Christ. This step continues until the end of our earthly life. Finally, at the coming of Christ, we will be glorified with him and the salvation process will be complete. Paul says that everything in the Christian's life during sanctification is used to conform them to the image of Christ. This includes suffering. If you are suffering for your faith, it is because God is using that suffering as part of your sanctification. Peter would say that suffering is an opportunity to prove your faith and give evidence to your sanctification,

"In [living hope through Christ] you rejoice, though now for a little while, if necessary, you have been grieved by various trials, so that the tested genuineness of your faith—more precious than gold that perishes though it is tested by fire—may be found to result in praise and glory and honor at the revelation of Jesus Christ." (1 Peter 1:7)

Peter viewed suffering as an opportunity to prove himself. Many of the early Christians felt very strongly about this. They were eager to prove how faithful they could be to Christ. We need to have a desire to prove ourselves. We modern American Christians have more opportunities to live out the gospel than any other group of Christians has seen. We can go anywhere we want in public and preach the gospel. We can gather as local assemblies without any fear. We can speak out on moral issues without retribution from the government. These freedoms are wonderful, but they have made us soft. We won't take a stand because we're scared of someone with an opposing view arguing with us and we panic at the mere thought of a legal battle over same-sex marriage. Christian, recognize where your hope is. Stop putting your hope in the temporal. When you truly grasp the security, we have in Christ for eternity your afflictions will begin to seem light and momentary.

Not only is suffering good for us as individuals, but it is also good for the church. If we had a wave of real persecution come through the Bible Belt, you could probably rip out the first and second chapter of this book. If your Christianity is only a set of values you hold to or just a part of your cultural upbringing, you won't stick around long during persecution. Once being a Christian is no longer advantageous, many church members will simply leave because it's not that important to them. Only the life-giving gospel and eternal hope of Christ will give you the perseverance to withstand suffering and stay true to your confession of Jesus Christ as Lord and Savior.

Suffering, while unpleasant, keeps the church pure. A church that is not persecuted, historically, is a church that becomes weak and compromising. The church in Rome is a perfect example of this. Prior to Constantine declaring Christianity the state religion in Rome, it was not easy being a Christian. The waves of persecution would normally weed out false professors because they could not withstand the suffering. For the most part, the unconverted Christians were not willing to stay in the church because they did not have the eternal hope and security of Christ. They did not have the truth of the gospel that would preserve them through the persecution. This kept the church relatively pure. There was heresy such as Gnosticism and Arianism that had to be combated, but false teachers didn't experience the comfort they do today. Once the persecution was gone and Christianity became culturally dominant, the church became very diluted. It was easy to be a Christian and therefore easy for unconverted Christians to hide within the church and never be challenged or tested. It was also much easier for false teachers to take root within the church. It is only by God's grace that His truth was preserved throughout dark times in the church such as this. It could have easily been lost. The same thing has happened with the American church. It is easy to be a Christian and so the church is filled with false professors and false teachers.

You may not like it, but the American church could use a healthy dose of persecution. Our need for purification has never been greater, and with our rapidly changing culture, we might begin to experience it to a degree. Are you ready? Our culture has made it easy for unconverted Christians to hide. We are a terrible representation of Christ to the world because many professing Christians are not in Christ. Suffering could do a great deal to remedy this. Suffering isn't what it used to be, but it should be. It shouldn't be something we run from or panic over. It should be viewed as a tool used by God to refine, test, and prepare his people. It should be seen as an opportunity to prove our devotion to the One that bore our guilt. Our Savior suffered for us, why should we not suffer for him?

WE'RE WRONG ABOUT OUR RIGHTS

I F THERE'S ONE thing Americans love, it's our rights. The Bill of Rights is one of the most cherished pieces of literature in American history. We hold it dear to our hearts. The first two amendments are especially important to us. Every good country boy owns a bible and a gun. I love the first and second amendments as much as any red-blooded American. However, there is a great deal of misunderstanding and idolization when it comes to American Christians and their "rights."

Freedom for All

Before I get into this, I want to make something clear. I am not attempting to make some kind of political statement. In fact, I am urging you to get away from a political mindset and focus more on the primary purpose of the church. American ideals have become so synonymous with Christianity that our purpose has been lost. We make moral stands based on political stances instead of making political stances based on moral convictions. We also believe our American rights are God-given even though God never promised us most of what we believe we are entitled to.

The first amendment is essential to the ideals our nation was built on. I love the first amendment. I also believe it is biblical. In 1 Timothy 2:1-2 Paul "urge[s] that supplications, prayers, intercessions, and thanksgivings be made for all people, for kings and all who are in high positions, that we may lead a peaceful and quiet life, godly, and dignified in every way." I would imagine this passage was on the minds of the Christians among our founding fathers. The first amendment grants this wish of Paul's. It gives Christians the ability to live according to God's word and preach his gospel without interference from the government. There is something about the amendment that many conservatives do not understand, however. It grants others the freedom to practice their religion too. A large number of conservatives draw the first amendment like a gun when they feel they are being challenged and shout their opponents down in its name. It would seem that they believe the first amendment only applies to Christians and those with conservative values. It doesn't.

It applies to all Americans. (Yes, liberals are notorious for this, but conservatives are equally as guilty) Because of this distortion of what the first amendment grants us, I believe it's important to discuss what it doesn't grant us.

The first amendment does not grant you the right to live in an echo chamber. What I mean by an echo chamber is, you are in a space in which everyone agrees with your personal beliefs and you are never confronted by an opposing view. Many conservatives want a place like this. In fact, a lot of conservatives are bigger "snowflakes" than the liberals they make fun of so much. They can't handle someone disagreeing with them, so they try to make the first amendment grant them something it was never intended to. This is important to understand. You have the right to stand on the street and preach the gospel. Mormons, Buddhists, and Muslims also have the right to stand on the street and preach next to you. We can say whatever we want, but others can say something in opposition to it as well.

Most conservatives are very hypocritical when it comes to this. They want the ability to promote Christian values, but they don't want anyone else to be allowed to promote a different set of values. I am not trying to promote non-Christian values, nor am I suggesting these false religions are preaching the same truth we are. The point I am trying to get across is, the first amendment does not guarantee Christians the right to live in some conservative eutopia where they are insulated from opposing world views and religions. Also, I don't believe we should even desire to live in such a place. Yes, I want the church to influence our culture in such a way that our communities have a large Christian population and Christian values are the norm, but I don't think we are called to place ourselves in a Christian bubble.

In Matthew 28:16-20, we see Jesus giving the Great Commission to the disciples. He charges them with going and making disciples. They were to go out into the culture and confront the world with the gospel. Guess what, this required the disciples to have nuanced conversations with people who held opposing world views. If the disciples would have been like many conservative Christians today, they would have simply moved to the country and lived out their days complaining to each other about how all these pagans are taking over the cities. They didn't do that. They understood that they were commanded to preach the gospel. They understood that meant they would face opposition. They understood they were not guaranteed the right to have everyone agree with them.

Christians are not given the right, by God or the government, to sit in their small rural communities and never come into contact with someone that is not a Christian. We are called to engage the culture. We should be excited to talk with a nonbeliever and articulate the gospel to them. We should be prepared to peacefully and thoughtfully oppose atheists. Stop thinking your rights are violated just because you come across someone that disagrees with you. If we exist within our Christian communities and never go outside their boundaries, we are holding the message of salvation captive. In Mark 2, Jesus was rebuked for eating with tax collectors. His response in verse 17 was, "Those that are well have no need of a physician, but those who are sick. I came not to call the righteous, but sinners." Jesus spent his entire life on earth confronting people with an opposing world view. He dedicated himself to sharing the life-changing message of the gospel with those that opposed him. Yet we believe we are entitled to sit happily in our bubble and never even meet a nonbeliever, much less have them openly disagree with us. We are keeping to ourselves, the very thing Jesus told us to give to the world. Don't get upset when you find yourself confronted by someone disagreeing with you. You were never promised anything else.

The reason so many conservative Christians have held so dearly to this distorted, hypocritical view of the first amendment is because they are lazy and nominal. They expect the government to spread Christianity for them. They want public schools to be strictly Christian. They want our laws to directly enforce Christian moral standards. They want all other religions forced out and forbade from practicing in public. They want this because they want the schools to disciple their kids, so they don't have to. Instead of confronting moral issues in the culture, they just want the government to get rid of the problem for them. Much of the conservative church is lazy, nominal, weak, and looking to the government to do its job. This is a horrible idea, however. The state church has never ended well. It has never been wise to attempt to create a "Christian" government, and it is not wise now.

The Problem with the State Church

There are two major problems that arise when a state church is created. The first major problem is, a state church always results in a shallow, fake Christianity. When Christian values are mandated by the government, we reach the height of moralism being substituted for the gospel. Everyone will act like a Christian, but almost no one will actually have a converted heart.

This happened in Rome when Christianity became the state-sponsored religion. As we have learned, prior to Constantine, the church was persecuted a great deal. The survival of the early church is really something to marvel at, and even more so when you consider the process in which one had to go through to be baptized and welcomed into the assembly. A believer that wanted to be baptized would have to go through lengthy training periods sometimes lasting three years before their baptism. The early church wanted to ensure that those it affirmed were converted Christians and had a solid grasp of the gospel. Because of the persecution by Rome and care taken by the early Christians, the unconverted church was not an issue like it would become after Constantine. Am I saying that every single person that professed Christ and identified with Christianity was a true convert? No. The visible church, consisting of everyone that professes Christ as Savior, will not be completely pure until Christ's return. However, the problem was not as bad as it is today.

When Constantine established Christianity as the state religion, everything changed for the church. It was now advantageous to be a Christian and problematic to not be one. Clergyman could become wealthy. Outspoken heretics could be exiled. It was a time in which, it seemed, everyone was a Christian. Churches exploded and grew exponentially. Because of the massive growth, new "converts" were not properly interviewed or trained and churches began to be filled with false professors. Because of the lack of persecution, they were able to stay hidden and never have their faith questioned or tested.

To a lesser degree, we can see this happening still today in small, rural, conservative communities across the country. In most of these communities, it is, to a degree, advantageous to display some sort of religious affiliation. An example of this I have seen time and time again is with high school football coaches. A new head coach will come to town and one of the first things he does is assure everyone that God and family come first. He does this because it is, most of the time, beneficial to his image in the community. It is usually followed by the use of foul language in front of student-athletes, a practice schedule that makes it difficult for players to attend mid-week services, and a work schedule that prevents his assistant coaches from going to church and spending time with their families on the weekends.

Now, not all football coaches are like this. In fact, I'm actually blaming you more than I am the ones that are like this. When conservative Christians create a culture that simply pays lip service to God but largely ignores him in their daily lives, scenarios like that head football coach are inevitable. We end up with a culture that identifies as Christian but knows nothing of true Christianity. What I have just described is a result of the culture mandating Christianity. Can you imagine if it was an actual state church? The problem would grow exponentially.

Fake Christianity is not the only problem with a state church. The other problem we have to consider is, governments change with the wind. Remember, before Rome fell in love with Christianity, it hated it. If we set a precedent that gives the state the right to mandate the religious beliefs of its citizens, we have to understand it could potentially turn on us. Politicians come and go. If the culture moves away from Christianity, like ours is, and you have given the government control of religion, the church now has to oppose the government and not just the culture. Government-mandated Christianity may seem like a dream, but it would soon become a nightmare.

You don't, or shouldn't, want a state church. You should want to see the church grow and God's word spread because of faithful followers of Christ having an impact on the world around them and people's hearts being changed by the gospel. I am not suggesting we completely remove ourselves from politics. We can vote for laws and people that align with God's moral standard. We should have a desire to see our legal system uphold the standard of morality given to us in God's word. We should not desire to abdicate our job as the church to the state. It robs us of our purpose and results in a fake, cultural Christianity. We have never been granted the right to be insulated from the opposition and we shouldn't view the first amendment, or the bible, as if they give us that right.

Come and Take Them

Before we get into this section, I want to reveal a little about myself. I love guns. I own several firearms. I am an avid hunter. I have a concealed carry permit and carry a handgun every day. I am a strong supporter of the second amendment and believe in the right to defend myself. I am with you. I am on your side when it comes to the gun debate. All that being said, I think we have lost our way in the midst of all the chaos surrounding the gun debate. Our guns have become idols. We worship the right to own them and believe Christians can't function properly without them. We need to be sure we keep our guns where they belong. Put them in a safe, gun rack, or holster on your belt, but don't put them on the throne of your life.

First of all, as I said, I believe the bible gives us the right to defend ourselves. The sixth commandment forbids murder, taking of innocent life, not killing, taking of life in general. There are times in which it is permitted to kill in order to protect innocent life. Psalm 82:3-4 is an exhortation to earthly rulers to take up for the weak and defenseless. Leaders, and anyone really, should have a desire to see justice carried out for those that cannot help themselves. Rescuing the weak from oppression will, at times, require force. In the 1940s, there was no talking things out with Hitler. If the Jews and millions of others in Europe were going to be rescued from the Nazi's, blood would have to be spilled. Human wickedness often requires life to be taken and given in order to stop evil from progressing. That's just the sad truth. Not only is this the case in global events, but it is also true with individuals. If my family is being threatened and there is a real possibility they will be killed by an attacker, I have a biblical right to take the life of the attacker in order to protect my family. Therefore, I believe in the right for all citizens to own firearms.

I believe Jesus himself clearly allows this right of defense of self and others as well. In Luke 22:35-38, we see an exchange between Jesus and his disciples shortly before his arrest and crucifixion.

"And he said to them, 'When I sent you out with no moneybag or knapsack or sandals, did you lack anything?' They said, 'Nothing.' He said to them, 'But now let the one who has a money bag take it, and likewise a knapsack. And let the one who has no sword sell his cloak and buy one. For I tell you that this Scripture must be fulfilled in me: "And he was numbered with the transgressors." For what is written about me has its fulfillment.' And they said, 'Look, Lord, here are two swords.' And he said to them, 'It is enough.'"

During his instructions, Jesus tells the disciples to sell their cloaks and buy a sword if they don't already have one. Many pacifists believe the term "sword" to be metaphorical and believe Jesus to be commanding the disciples to arm themselves spiritually. However, the money bag and knapsack are literal, so it would be logical for the sword to be literal. Also, the fact that the disciples possess swords, to begin with, proves that Jesus did not condemn defensive weapons. He even affirms it when the two swords are presented to him. The point I'm trying to get at is, yes, I believe the bible gives people the right to possess defensive weapons and use those weapons to defend themselves and their loved ones, even if that means taking a life.

Conservative gun owners are probably really on board so far. You might have even shouted "amen" as you read the previous paragraph. I would like to take a moment to tip my hat to pacifists for a moment though. When I say pacifist, I mean someone who is opposed to owning a weapon based on their religious convictions. I would not agree with a pacifist that believes the Bible forbids Christians from owning weapons or defending themselves. However, I do think it is very noble and humble for a Christian to choose to surrender their right to self-defense if they believe it glorifies God. Let us not forget, while Jesus affirms the right to self-defense in Luke 22:35-38, a few verses later in 22:47-53 he orders his disciples to stand down as he forfeits his own right to self-defense. Jesus chose to subject himself to the cruelties of his enemies for the sake of his people. If his followers choose to follow this example and lay down their arms, who are we to scoff at them? Pacifists should not be viewed as weak or stupid. Their meekness and humility are actually quite noble. Gun-toting conservatives could learn from them.

The death-grip many conservatives have on their guns is not biblical or becoming of a Christian. Yes, I believe we are allowed to defend ourselves, but the obsession we have with our guns has become idolatrous and sinful. I know many conservatives cling to their guns because they believe without them the government will force its liberal ideals on us and our nation will be lost. If that is the first thing your mind goes to you should read chapters 3 and 4 again. An over-attachment to our guns reveals that we are refusing to submit to suffering that God has ordained for us and we are concerned more about the survival of the nation than following Jesus.

We have to maintain a proper perspective on gun ownership. Yes, Jesus affirmed the disciples owning swords. However, if you look at the passage in Luke 22:35-38, he says that two swords are enough for 12 men.

What are we to take from this? In the United States, there are more guns than people and Jesus is saying a dozen men can get by with just two swords. I believe what Jesus is implying is, while we have the right to self-defense, we should not obsess over it. There is nothing Christian about arming yourself to the teeth. Jesus is not proud of your basement full of rifles and ammo cans. You're not advancing God's kingdom by carrying a Glock 19 and 4 spare mags every day. Defend yourself, but don't obsess over it. Don't forget God is still in control and when it's your time to go, your gun collection isn't going to change his plans.

I am not trying to make a political statement in support of gun control. I am a strong supporter of the second amendment and will always vote to maintain the rights that it gives us. That being said, it is foolish for Christians to proudly announce their plans to defy the government if stronger gun control laws are put into place. Hear me out on this. When someone defies the United States government, there are only two ways that can go. You will be arrested or killed. Those are the only two logical ends if you choose to go up against the government.

Now, I have no problem being imprisoned or killed for something worthwhile. I believe it would be a tremendous honor for it to be said that I gave my life for the gospel of Jesus Christ. That is a legacy I would love to leave for my children. I have no desire, however, for my legacy to be that I gave up my life so a bunch of guys in MAGA hats can keep their ARs. So no, I would not defy the government if they came after our guns. I would comply with their demands, understanding gun ownership is not essential to my Christianity, and continue preaching the gospel and accept whatever God has in store for me after that.

Again, I'm not attempting to make this about politics, and I am not suggesting we need more gun control. I am simply trying to change the perspective of Christians and guns. You can buy guns and you can defend yourself, but don't allow the right to do these things to become an idol. Advancing God's kingdom through the spread of the gospel is our singular purpose. Stay focused on that purpose and keep guns where they belong.

WHITE-WASHED CHRISTIANITY

I F YOU WERE to travel across the Bible Belt and visit all the conservative protestant churches, you would find that segregation is at its height on Sunday mornings. The truth is, most conservative Protestant churches have little to no diversity. There are many reasons for this, but the primary reason, I believe, is a subtle, and sometimes not so subtle, remnant of racism left over from decades of cultural conditioning. No, there are no institutional forms of racism in which minorities are barred from attending white churches or anything of that nature. However, the attitudes and behaviors of many conservative whites toward minorities are enough to drive a wedge between ethnic groups and create a white-washed Christianity.

The New Social Justice Movement

Before I get into the issue of conservatism lacking diversity, I would like to take a moment to discuss the modern social justice movement. I don't want what I say here to be used as fuel for a liberal, anti-gospel argument. I fully reject the teachings of this new social justice movement that is sweeping the country. This is a movement built on ideas such as critical race theory and intersectionality. It is not Christian and leaves no room for the reconciling work of the gospel. I am going to try my hardest to represent this movement and these ideas as accurately as possible because I don't want to simply build straw men to be easily torn down. I have studied these arguments and sincerely hope I am not doing a disservice to those that hold to them by misrepresenting them. All that being said, here it goes.

Critical race theory and intersectionality teach that there is, in our society, an oppressing class. This group of people is oppressive simply because of who they are. It is not necessary for them to actively engage in physical oppression, they are oppressive by simply existing. This class, in our society, has been identified as the middle to upper class straight white male. These men are considered oppressors simply because of who they are. People that are not in this class are all oppressed to some degree. The degree to which one is oppressed is dependent on the number of variances by which they differ from this oppressive class. A middle to upper class straight white female is slightly oppressed because she is a female. A lower-class lesbian black female is considered extremely oppressed. Do you see how this works? The farther away a person is from identifying with the oppressive class, the more oppressed they are. Just like the oppressors don't actually have to do anything oppressive to be considered oppressive, the oppressed don't actually have to experience oppression to be considered oppressed. Oppression is not defined as a physical domineering of one person over another but by a perceived difference in opportunity and privilege.

Once everyone is properly identified according to their degree of oppression, the application of this modern social justice movement can begin. According to critical race theory, the ultimate good is for oppression to be battled against leading to the oppressors being oppressed. It is considered right and moral for the "oppressed" to rise up against their "oppressors" and remove them from power. So, removing all middle to upper class straight white males from any position of authority simply because they are middle to upper class straight white males is considered a good thing. The only way to bring justice to the oppressed is to attack the oppressor. This modern wave of social justice warriors wants to see white government officials, businessmen, and even ministers removed from their positions and replaced with someone from an "oppressed" people group in order to truly achieve justice. There are three major problems with this movement and its ideas.

The first problem is that it requires no actual oppression to take place. The varying groups of oppressors and the oppressed are identified by perceived oppression, not actual oppression. Straight white males don't have to actually do anything to be considered oppressive. I am in support of standing against injustice and oppression. I find it absolutely deplorable that it took until 1965 for all citizens to be allowed to vote in this country. I am glad there were people willing to stand up against that kind of systematic and institutional oppression and racism. When that kind of injustice is present within the culture, I would sincerely hope all Christians would actively take a stand against it. However, this new social justice movement is attacking institutions and individuals based on perceived oppression, not actual oppression. They want business and government leaders removed, not because they have done anything wrong, but simply because they're white. Innocent people are being attacked based on their skin color. It seems ironic, doesn't it? That is the teaching of critical race theory. The ultimate good is to oppress the "oppressor."

The second major problem with the modern social justice movement is that it does not provide any possibility for reconciliation. The ultimate good is oppressing the oppressors, but do the oppressed eventually become the oppressors? Not according to this theory. There is no end game with critical race theory. There is not a goal of reconciliation. All it provides is a hostility towards those that are considered to be oppressors and the only remedy is to attack and oppress them. This is extremely anti-gospel. The gospel brings about reconciliation. Yes, oppressors should be confronted and called to repentance, but the oppressed are called to forgive. Past sins are to be forgotten and a newfound love and respect should take their place. The gospel calls us to move on from injustice, not simply reverse it.

Not only is reconciliation impossible between the oppressor and the oppressed, intersectionality causes division between the varying oppressed groups. Someone can always find another characteristic that makes them more oppressed than someone else. There is no end to the divisions that can take place when intersectionality is applied. Instead of finding our identity in Christ and being unified in that identity, intersectionality promotes the use of self-identity to create more division. This kind of divisive and problematic mindset is not consistent with the gospel and its call for reconciliation.

The gospel message demands that Christians confront injustice with the goal of reconciliation. Our ultimate goal should not be to simply topple the current power structure but to bring people together in a union with Christ. Paul makes this clear in Colossians 3:11 when he says, "here there is not Greek and Jew, circumcised and uncircumcised, barbarian, Scythian, slave, free; but Christ is all, and in all." The Jews of Paul's day would have looked upon the Greeks with disdain. They would have considered them lawless and heathen. Similarly, the Greeks would have looked upon a barbarian or Scythian with a scoff. These lowly people were rough and uneducated in Greek culture. Notice, there is no call for the barbarians or Scythians to topple the power structure of their culture and society. There is only a call to become unified in Christ. Injustice must be dealt with, but it must be dealt with in a gospel-centered manner that desires reconciliation.

The third major issue with the modern social justice movement and its application are that it does not take into consideration the heart. This modern movement seeks to attack racism and bigotry at the institutional level. The problem is, that battle has already been won. Businesses and government entities are not allowed to be systematically racist. They can get into a great deal of trouble for discrimination. Am I saying racism is not an issue in the United States? No, it is still an issue, but it is a heart issue. Racism and bigotry are symptoms of a sinful heart. Replacing leaders and attacking institutions are not going to change someone's heart. They're fighting the wrong fight. Only the gospel can truly bring reconciliation and justice because, as the old saying goes, "the ground is level at the cross."

You Can't Erase the Past or Lines on a Map

While I whole-heartedly reject the ideas behind the modern social justice movement, I believe there is an obvious problem of racism remaining in the hearts of many white Christian conservatives. Let's just be honest, conservative Protestantism is very white, and it's not because minorities don't want sound biblical doctrine. It's because they don't feel welcome or accepted in our churches. I could write a whole series of books on the ways racism and prejudice manifest themselves, but I'm just going to mention a few here that will, hopefully, make you examine your own heart and actions.

The first way white conservatives reveal their remnant of racism is the attempt to ignore, and essentially erase, the past atrocities that African Americans have experienced throughout the existence of this country. Yes, I do believe we should strive for reconciliation and try to put past sins behind us as we unite in the name of Jesus, but that doesn't mean we can totally forget about what happened. We have to be sensitive to the fact that a history of slavery and bigotry has had huge effects on individuals and on cultures as a whole. I hear white conservatives shout all the time, "I never owned a slave, and you were never a slave." Yes, you're right. You have never owned a human being, and African Americans in the United States today have never been owned as slaves. However, they can read history books and understand that, just a few generations ago, their ancestors were considered no more valuable than livestock just because of their skin color. Even young African American kids today have grandparents that can remember a time they were not allowed to vote because of their skin color.

Our nation has a long history of bigotry and hatred toward African Americans and they have suffered as a whole for generations. Even today African Americans are much more likely to come from single-parent homes and live in poverty than whites. Black children typically have fewer opportunities for higher education than white children. The result of our nation's bigotry is that the black community does not have access to many of the privileges and opportunities that the white community does. For affluent white conservatives to scoff at the suggestion of us owing the black community an apology or simply recognizing the damage we have done as a nation is to reveal how little you actually care about your fellow image-bearer.

This was seen in 1995 when the Southern Baptist Convention released an official stand against racism as well as an apology to the African American community. The SBC was founded because there was a large group of Baptists in the 1800s that wanted to keep their slaves.

Even after slavery was ended a large number of SBC churches would not allow African Americans to attend services. Do you understand that? Professing Christians, possessing the true knowledge of Jesus Christ, were withholding that knowledge from an entire population because of their skin color. We owed them an apology. However, there were many people in the SBC who were not fond of the release. They did not believe an apology or statement of any kind on racism was necessary. That is because they did not want to bear the guilt of racism and would rather attempt to erase the past. If we are not willing to apologize on behalf of our nation or denomination, or at least recognize the damage that has been done, we will never be reconciled with our African American brothers and sisters.

Another avenue by which prejudice works its way out is by belittling cultures and making blanket statements about people that look alike. Racial jokes are not uncommon in the white community. If a joke is made about African Americans, it usually includes fried chicken, watermelon, saggy pants, rap music, or some other stereotype. The statement these kinds of jokes make is, "I don't really care about who you are, because of your skin color I'm going to assume these characteristics about you and make a mockery of you and the culture I assume you come from." Please, if you are a professing Christian, rise above this. Have some respect for your fellow image-bearers and desire to know and understand them for who they are.

Not only do many white conservatives belittle cultures through distasteful jokes, but they also make blanket statements and assumptions based on what people look like and ignore the diversity found in certain parts of the world. This is seen all the time with people from Asia, the Middle East, and Central and South America. There are many different countries and cultures within each of these regions. However, many white conservatives view them as all the same. They don't care if someone is from Afghanistan or Pakistan. They don't care if someone is from China or Japan. They don't care if someone is from Mexico or Guatemala. To them, there is no distinction. They are simply Middle Eastern or Arab, Asian, or Mexican. They don't care to actually learn about the individual and where they come from. This attitude completely rejects the culture and identity of a person. It tells minorities that, "I don't care who you are or where you come from. You look and talk like 'this' so I'm going to assume 'this' about you." It totally devalues your fellow image-bearer and makes them instantly feel unwelcomed and unwanted, and for good reason. Take time to actually learn about people and get to know them. Have a desire to understand their culture, and their perspective of our society.

Subtle Supremacy

"White supremacist" is a term that carries a lot of weight and I do not throw it around casually. Therefore, I will not be referring to anyone as a white supremacist in this book. There are a great number of white conservatives though that have subtle behaviors that reveal a certain arrogance when they compare themselves to minorities. One of the ways this manifests itself is when a white person refers to a member of a minority as "a good one." What does that even mean? They would never refer to another white person as "one of the good ones." What many people mean by this statement is, in their mind, an individual has risen above their lesser culture and actually become a quality citizen. The "good one" probably behaves and dresses similarly to them so they are slightly better than the rest of their race. This attitude is detestable because it assumes that minorities have to meet some standard before they can be welcomed or considered equals. White conservatives have to be more aware of what their language reveals about their heart. If you are setting standards and making distinctions based on someone's race and culture and degrading them for not behaving or looking like you, your heart is not where it needs to be.

Sadly, the church itself is promoting subtle forms of racism and white arrogance. In most small towns across the South and in other rural areas, white Protestant conservatives have very little interaction with minorities. The interaction they do have is almost always in the form of aid. Perhaps it is a service project in which the youth group goes to the inner city and fixes up dilapidated buildings or works in a soup kitchen. Or, maybe the church goes on a mission trip to a foreign country and gives medical aid or digs water wells. Don't get me wrong, activities like this are good. We should have a heart for people in need and want to help them. However, for many small-town churchgoers, this is the only exposure to minorities they will ever have. Every time they encounter someone of a different race, they are helping them.

What this eventually does is develop a mindset that these people are helpless and cannot make it without us. They are never viewed as equals. These same churches that go on these mission trips never have a black guest preacher. Their students never, as equals, intermingle with students that look different than them. There is never any interaction in which minorities are viewed as equals. They are always the people we are having to help. Church leaders should bring in speakers and preachers that are of different ethnicities than you. Create events in which your church engages with minorities as equals. Stop creating this cycle in which we teach our children that minorities are simply the people we have to continuously help. Start creating an environment in which they are viewed as fellow image-bearers of God and our brothers and sisters in Christ.

Let Them Come

Whether it is immigrants from Central and South America crossing our Southern border or refugees from the Middle East and other places overseas, most conservatives don't want foreigners here. There are three aspects of the harsh conservative stance that greatly concern me. When conservative Christians get red-faced and belligerent over immigration, they reveal an arrogance about their nationality, lack of compassion, and a lack of gospel-centeredness.

Let's make one thing clear, you did absolutely nothing to deserve being born in the United States. God, in His grace, chose to place you in this country with the freedoms you enjoy, and his grace is the only reason you are here. You have no right to proclaim that another human being doesn't "deserve" to be here. This attitude is no different than the attitude of many of the religious bigots Jesus encountered in his earthly ministry. They believed their Jewish heritage made them better than the Greeks or any other non-Jews. Jesus and his apostles denounced this mindset. John says in 1 John 2:2 that "He is the propitiation for our sins, and not for ours only but also for the sins of the whole world." John is saying that Jesus' blood is not efficient for Jews only, but for people of all ethnicities. Everyone is sinful and in need of the grace of God. No people group or ethnic group is worthy of anything that another is not. I understand that national security is important, and we need to protect our borders, but there is nothing Christian about you believing another person doesn't deserve to stand on the same ground as you.

Pride and arrogance are major issues, but they are not nearly as ugly as the hatefulness and lack of compassion exhibited by conservative Christians in the immigration debate. Again, I understand that national security is important. I do not envy the men and women that are in charge of keeping us safe. They have a difficult job and are forced to make really tough decisions that they have to live with. That being said, it should never seem good to a follower of Jesus Christ when a family is torn apart at the border. It should never seem good that a family is desperate to flee a war-torn country overseas and has nowhere to go. We should not celebrate these things or act as if they are inconsequential. Where is your compassion for fellow image-bearers? People in Central and South America spend their life savings and risk their lives to simply have an opportunity to be in the United States. People in Middle Eastern countries are being attacked mercilessly and cry out for help.

I get it, we have laws and protocols and those things keep us safe. But let the state take care of our borders and let the love of Christ compel his church to have compassion for people who are suffering and in need.

God gives a command to the Israelites in Deuteronomy 10:19 to "love the sojourners . . . for you were sojourners in the land of Egypt." The context of this verse is God commanding the Israelites to have a heart that is pure and full of love for him. A symptom of a heart that loves God is love for others. The Israelites were to show compassion to troubled foreigners because they had experienced so much grace and compassion themselves in their rescue from Egypt. If someone has truly experienced the love and mercy of God, that love should overflow to others that are in need of grace and mercy.

Finally, does the gospel ever cross your mind when you whole-heartedly reject these immigrants and refugees? Think about it, if I were to get on a plane and fly to Syria and begin to preach the gospel of Jesus Christ, what would happen? I've never been to Syria so I really can't say, but I would imagine there would be a great deal of hostility. I would imagine that imprisonment, bodily harm, and maybe even death would be a real possibility. However, if there were Syrian refugees that landed on our shores or in our airports, I would then be able to witness to those people without any fear of harm. Refugees and immigrants coming to our country give us an opportunity to preach the gospel to people we would otherwise never be able to reach. Sadly, most conservative American Christians miss that blessing because they are more concerned with maintaining the nation and their comfort than they are sharing the gospel. Stop viewing everything through the lens of a nationalist and start viewing things through the lens of the gospel.

Whether it is immigrants, refugees, or minorities currently living in our communities, we have to do better at reaching out to them, as equals, and sharing the love of Christ. Examine your heart. Be brave enough to confront your own bigotry and arrogance. Desire reconciliation with your brothers and sisters in Christ. Allow the gospel to stir up your compassion for others. Seek to be united in the name of Jesus.

CONCLUSION

I KNOW THIS BOOK has not been an easy one. There have been toes stepped on and egos bruised. I hope you understand these words have been written out of love and hope to see the gospel transform lives. I dearly love the religious conservative movement and its commitment to orthodoxy. However, we are not perfect. We have a lot we need to work on. I hope you will take what is written in this book and apply it and examine your own heart and life. I pray that God will use it to give you a passion for the gospel and sharing the love of Jesus to those around you.

This book is meant to be concise and is, by no means, a comprehensive discussion on its topics. It is only meant to be the first swipe at ripping off the mask that is American Christianity. My hope is that it spurs on further study. I hope you gain a desire to diligently seek out the truth and further God's kingdom. That being said, I would like to leave you with some suggested resources that deal with the topics discussed in this book. I hope they will help you to be rooted in biblical truth and put an end to the American Masquerade.

Suggested Resources: Some good books to read would be, The Explicit Gospel by Matt Chandler, Church Membership by Jonathon Leeman, The Last Days According to Jesus by R.C. Sproul, Radical and Counter-Culture by David Platt, and Under Our Skin by Benjamin Watson. Russell Moore has a very insightful article called "What a stupid bumper sticker can tell us about American Christianity." He also has two excellent videos on YouTube entitled, "Why Christians should fight for religious liberties of false religions" and "Dr. Russell Moore responds to question at SBC16." Jeff Durbin and Apologia Studios have some wonderful resources in the form of podcasts and YouTube videos. I hope these resources will help you in your sanctification and walk with the Lord.